THURMOND PUBLIC LIBRARY.
Sewanee, Tennessee

SEWANEE

SEWANEE

BY

WILLIAM ALEXANDER PERCY

INTRODUCTION BY
WALKER PERCY

ILLUSTRATED BY
KATHARINE PETTIGREW

FREDERIC C. BEIL
NEW YORK
1982

From
Lanterns on the Levee
by William Alexander Percy.
Copyright 1941 by Alfred A. Knopf, Inc.,
and renewed 1969 by LeRoy Pratt Percy.
Reprinted by permission of Alfred A. Knopf, Inc.

Introduction copyright © 1973, 1982,
by Walker Percy.
Reprinted by permission of
Louisiana State University Press.

Copyright © 1982 by Walker Percy
Library of Congress Catalog Card Number 82-60214
ISBN 0-913720-37-2
All rights reserved
Printed in the United States of America

INTRODUCTION

I REMEMBER the first time I saw him. I was thirteen and he had come to visit my mother and me and my brothers in Athens, Georgia, where we were living with my grandmother after my father's death.

We had heard of him, of course. He was the fabled relative, the one you liked to speculate about. His father was a United States senator and he had been a decorated infantry officer in World War I. Besides that, he was a poet. The fact that he was also a lawyer and a planter didn't cut much ice— after all, the South was full of lawyer-planters. But how many people did you know who were war heroes and wrote books of poetry? One had heard of Rupert Brooke and Joyce Kilmer, but they were dead.

The curious fact is that my recollection of him

even now, after meeting him, after living in his house for twelve years, and now thirty years after his death, is no less fabled than my earliest imaginings. The image of him that takes form in my mind still owes more to Rupert Brooke and those photographs of young English officers killed in Flanders than to a flesh-and-blood cousin from Greenville, Mississippi.

I can only suppose that he must have been, for me at least, a personage, a presence, radiating that mysterious quality we call charm, for lack of a better word, in such high degree that what comes to mind is not that usual assemblage of features and habits which make up our memories of people but rather a quality, a temper, a set of mouth, a look through the eyes.

For his eyes were most memorable, a piercing gray-blue and strangely light in my memory, as changeable as shadows over water, capable of passing in an instant, we were soon to learn, from merriment—he told the funniest stories we'd ever heard—to a level gray gaze cold with reproof. They were beautiful and terrible eyes, eyes to be careful around. Yet now, when I try to remember them, I cannot see them otherwise than as shadowed by sadness.

What we saw at any rate that sunny morning in Georgia in 1930, and what I still vividly remember, was a strikingly handsome man, slight of build and quick as a youth. He was forty-five then, an advanced age, one would suppose, to a thirteen-year-old, and gray-haired besides, yet the abiding impression was of a youthfulness—and an exoticness. He had in fact just returned from the South Seas—this was before the jet age and I'd never heard of anybody going there but Gauguin and Captain Bligh—where he had lived on the beach at Bora Bora.

He had come to invite us to live with him in Mississippi. We did, and upon my mother's death not long after, he adopted me and my two brothers. At the time what he did did not seem remarkable. What with youth's way of taking life as it comes—how else can you take it when you have no other life to compare it with?—and what with youth's incapacity for astonishment or gratitude, it did not seem in the least extraordinary to find oneself orphaned at fifteen and adopted by a bachelor-poet-lawyer-planter and living in an all-male household visited regularly by other poets, politicians, psychiatrists, sociologists, black preachers, folk singers, itinerant harmonica players. One friend came to seek advice on a book he wanted to write and stayed a year to write it. It was, his house, a standard stopover for all manner of people who were trying to "understand the South," that perennial American avocation, and whether or not they succeeded, it was as valuable to me to try to understand them as to be understood. The observers in this case were at least as curious a phenomenon as the observed.

Now belatedly I can better assess what he did for us and I even have an inkling what he gave up to do it. For him, to whom the world was open and who felt more at home in Taormina than in Jackson—for though he loved his home country, he had to leave it often to keep loving it—and who in fact could have stayed on at Bora Bora and chucked it all like Gauguin (he told me once he was tempted), for him to have taken on three boys, age fourteen, thirteen, and nine, and raised them, amounted to giving up the freedom of bachelorhood and taking on the burden of parenthood without the consolations of marriage. Gauguin chucked it all, quit, cut out and went to the islands for the sake of art and became a great painter if not a great human being. Will Percy not only did not chuck anything; he shouldered somebody else's burden. Fortunately for us, he did not subscribe to Faulkner's precept that a good poem is worth any number of old ladies—for if grandmothers are dispensable, why not second cousins? I don't say we did him in (he would laugh at that), but he didn't write much poetry afterwards and he died young. At any rate, whatever he lost or gained in the transaction, I know what I gained: a vocation and in a real sense a second self, that is, the work and the self which, for better or worse, would not otherwise have been open to me.

For to have lived in Will Percy's house, with "Uncle Will" as we called him, as a raw youth from age fourteen to twenty-six, a youth whose only talent was a knack for looking and listening, for tuning in and soaking up, was nothing less than to be informed in the deepest sense of the word. What was to be listened to, dwelled on, pondered over for the next thirty years was of course the man himself, the unique human being, and when I say unique I mean it in its most literal sense: he was one of a kind: I never met anyone remotely like him. It was to encounter a complete, articulated view of the world as tragic as it was noble. It was to be introduced to Shakespeare, to Keats, to Brahms, to Beethoven—and unsuccessfully, it

[xi]

turned out, to Wagner whom I never liked, though I was dragged every year to hear Flagstad sing Isolde—as one seldom if ever meets them in school.

"Now listen to this part," he would say as Gluck's *Orfeo* played—the old 78s not merely dropped from a stack by the monstrous Capehart, as big as a sideboard, but then picked up and turned over by an astounding hoop-like arm—and you'd make the altogether unexpected discovery that music, of all things, can convey the deepest and most unnameable human feelings and give great pleasure in doing so.

Or: "Read this," and I'd read or, better still, he'd read aloud, say, Viola's speech to Olivia in *Twelfth Night*:

> Make me a willow cabin at your gate,
> And call upon my soul within the house;
>
> .   .   .   .
>
> And make the babbling gossip of the air
> Cry out "Olivia!"

You see? he'd as good as say, and what I'd begin to see, catch on to, was the great happy reach and play of the poet at the top of his form.

For most of us, the communication of beauty takes two, the teacher and the hearer, the pointer and the looker. The rare soul, the Wolfe or Faulkner, can assault the entire body of literature single-handedly. I couldn't or wouldn't. I had a great teacher. The teacher points and says *Look;* the response is *Yes, I see.*

But he was more than a teacher. What he was to me was a fixed point in a confusing world. This is not to say I always took him for my true north and set my course accordingly. I did not. But even when I did not follow him, it was usually in *relation* to him, whether with him or against him, that I defined myself and my own direction. Perhaps he would not have had it differently. Surely it is the highest tribute to the best people we know to use them as best we can, to become, not their disciples, but ourselves.

It is the good fortune of those who did not know him that his singular charm, the unique flavor of the man, transmits with high fidelity in *Lanterns on the Levee* (1941), which includes the chapter "Sewanee," published herewith. His gift for communicating, communicating himself, an enthusiasm, a sense of beauty, moral outrage, carries over faithfully to the cold printed page, although for those who did not know him the words cannot evoke—or can they?—the mannerisms, the quirk of mouth, the shadowed look, the quick Gallic shrug, the inspired flight of eyebrows at an absurdity, the cold Anglo-Saxon gaze. (For he was this protean: one time I was reading *Ivanhoe*, the part about the fight between Richard and Saladin, and knowing Richard was one of Uncle Will's heroes, I identified one with the other. But wait: wasn't he actually more like Saladin, not the sir-knight defender of the Christian West but rather the subtle easterner, noble in his own right? I didn't ask him, but if I had, he'd have probably shrugged: both, neither. . . .)

It should be noted that despite conventional assessments of *Lanterns on the Levee* as an expression of the "aristocratic" point of view of the Old South, Will Percy had no use for genealogical games, the old Southern itch for coats of arms and tracing back connections to the English squire-archy. Indeed if I know anything at all about Will Percy, I judge that in so far as there might be a connection between him and the Northumberland Percys, they, not he, would have to claim kin. He made fun of his ancestor Don Carlos, and if he claimed Harry Hotspur, it was a kinship of spirit. His own aristocracy was a meritocracy of character, talent, performance, courage, and quality of life.

[xiv]

It is just that, a person and a life, which comes across in *Sewanee*. And about him I will say no more than that he was the most extraordinary man I have ever known and that I owe him a debt which cannot be paid.

SEWANEE

I HAD been exposed to enough personalities mellow and magnificent to educate a Hottentot and in the process I had somehow received enough formal instruction to condition me for college. Fafar and his brothers had gone to Princeton, Father and his brothers to Sewanee (The University of the South, an Episcopal institution) and to Virginia Law School. Where I should go no one knew, least of all myself, so because it was fairly near and healthy and genteel and inexpensive, Father and Mother drew a long sigh, set me on the train bound for Sewanee, and betook themselves to Europe with Mr. Cook, on their first foreign tour. I was fifteen plus one month, in short trousers, small, weakly, self-reliant, and ignorant as an egg. I had the dimmest notion of how children were born though I knew it required a little co-operation; I had never heard of fraternities, I had never read a football score, I had never known a confidant or been in love. My instructions had been to enter the preparatory school, which was military, but I watched the grammar-school boys in their dusty ill-kept uniforms and I suspected they smelled bad. I developed an antipathy to the military life—which I've never overcome—and so, to the astonishment of the college authorities, I presented myself to them for entrance exams, and passed.

By no means brilliant, I studied hard, often getting up at six, to the scandal of other students, to struggle with Latin and math, and I made excellent grades. I don't know why I studied hard, but I had no shadow of a doubt it was the thing to do. English was my favorite course, whether because of the huge undigested gobs of the best I'd already read or because of Dr. Henneman, it would be hard to guess. He was passionate, black-bearded, bespectacled, with an adoration for *Beowulf*, Chaucer, Shakespeare, a grimace for Dr. Donne and the metaphysical school (oh, woeful unshakable influence), and, much more important, a capacity for furious moral tantrums in which, his beard on end clear out to his ears, he would beat the desk with his fist and roar:

"My God, gentlemen, *do* something!" We earnestly intended to, after such a scene.

And the other great course of those days was Dr. DuBose's Ethics. He was a tiny silver saint who lived elsewhere, being more conversant with the tongues of angels than of men. Sometimes sitting on the edge of his desk in his black gown, talking haltingly of Aristotle, he would suspend, rapt, in some mid air beyond our ken, murmuring: "The starry heavens—" followed by indefinite silence. We, with a glimpse of things, would tiptoe out of the classroom, feeling luminous, and never knowing when he returned to time and space.

It was a small college, in wooded mountains, its students drawn from the impoverished Episcopal gentry of the South, its boarding-houses and dormitories presided over by widows of bishops and Confederate generals. Great Southern names were thick—Kirby-Smith, Elliott, Quintard, Polk, Gorgas, Shoup, Gailor. The only things it wasn't rich in were worldly goods, sociology, and science. A place to be hopelessly sentimental about and to unfit one for anything except the good life.

Until I came to Sewanee I had been utterly without intimates of my own age. I had liked children whose pleasures were my pleasures, but they had not been persons to me and had left no mark. Here I suddenly found myself a social being, among young creatures of charm and humor, more experienced than I, but friendly and fascinating. I was never generally popular, but I had more than my share of friends. I am never surprised at people liking me, I'm always surprised if they don't. I like them and, if they don't like me, I feel they've made a mistake, they've misunderstood something. There's so much backing and filling about getting acquainted—indirection confuses and sometimes deceives me.

Probably because of my size and age and length of trouser I was plentifully adopted. It is a long time now: some of them have gone the journey, others have fallen by the road and can't go on and are just waiting, and a few have won through to autumn. But then the springtime was on them and they taught and tended me in the greenwoods as the Centaurs did Achilles—I don't know how I ever recovered to draw my own bow. Percy

Huger, noble and beautiful like a sleepy St. Bernard; Elliott Cage, full of dance-steps and song-snatches, tender and protective, and sad beneath; Paul Ellerbe, who first read me *Dover Beach*, thereby disclosing the rosy mountain-ranges of the Victorians; Harold Abrams, dark and romantic with his violin, quoting the *Rubáiyát* and discoursing Shaw; Parson Masterson, jostling with religion, unexpected and quaint; Sinkler Manning, a knight who met a knight's death at Montfaucon; Arthur Gray, full of iridescence, discovering new paths and views in the woods and the world; Huger Jervey, brilliant and bumptious then, brilliant and wise now, and so human; and more, many more, all with gifts they shared with me, all wastrel creditors who never collected. Peace to them, and endless gratitude.

I suppose crises occurred, problems pressed, decisions had to be made, those four shining years, but for me only one altered the sunlight. Once a month I would ride ten miles down the wretched mountain road to Winchester, go to confession, hear mass, and take communion. I had been thinking, I had never stopped thinking, I was determined to be honest if it killed me. So I knelt in the little Winchester church examining my conscience and preparing for confession. How it came about did not seem sudden or dramatic or anything but sad. As I started to the confessional I knew there was no use going, no priest could absolve me, no church could direct my life or my judgment, what most believed I could not believe. What belief remained there was no way of gauging yet. I only knew there was an end, I could no longer pretend to myself or cry: "Mea culpa. Help Thou mine unbelief." It was over, and forever. I rode back to the leafy mountain mournful and unregretful, knowing thenceforth I should breathe a starker and a colder air, with no place to go when I was tired. I would be getting home to the mountain, but for some things there was no haven, the friendly Centaurs couldn't help: from now on I would be living with my own self.

There's no way to tell of youth or of Sewanee, which is youth, directly; it must be done obliquely and by parable. I come back to the mountain often and see with a pang, however different it may be to me, it is no different, though Huger and Sinkler and I are forgotten. Then with humility I try to blend and merge the past and the present, to reach the unchanging essence. To my heart the essence, the unbroken melodic theme, sounds something like this:

The college has about three hundred young men or inmates, or students as they are sometimes called, and besides, quite a number of old ladies, who always were old and ladies, and who never die. It's a long way away, even from Chattanooga, in the middle of woods, on top of a bastion of mountains crenelated with blue coves. It is so beautiful that people who have once been there always, one way or another, come back. For such as can detect apple green in an evening sky, it is Arcadia—not the one that never used to be, but the one that many people always live in; only this one can be shared.

In winter there is a powder of snow; the pines sag like ladies in ermine, and the other trees are glassy and given to creaking. Later, arbutus is under the dead leaves where they have drifted, but unless you look for it be-times, you'll find instead puffs of ghost caught under the higher trees, and that's dogwood, and puffs of the saddest color in the world that's tender too, and that's redbud, which some say is pink and some purple and some give up but simply must write a poem about. The rest of the flowers you wouldn't believe in if I told you, so I'll tell you: anemones and hepaticas and blood-root that troop under the cliffs, always together, too ethereal to mix with reds and yellows or even pinks; and violets everywhere, in armies. The gray and purple and blue sort you'll credit, but not the tiny yellow ones with the bronze throats, nor the jack-rabbit ones with royal purple ears and faces of pale lavender that stare without a bit of violet modesty. If you've seen azalea —and miscalled it wild honeysuckle, probably—you still don't know what it is unless you've seen it here, with its incredible range of color from white through shell pink to deep coral (and now and then a tuft of orange that doesn't match anything else in the whole woods), and its perfume actually dangerous, so pagan it is. After it you'd better hunt for a calacanthus with brown petals (what else likes its petal brown?) and a little melancholy in its scent, to sober you. We call our bluets "innocence," for that's what they are. They troop near the iris, which when coarsened by gardens some call fleur-de-lis, and others, who care nothing about names, flags. Our orchids we try to make respectable by christening them "lady-slippers," but they still look as if they had been designed by D. H. Lawrence—only they're rose- and canary-colored.

After Orion has set—in other words, when the most fragile and delicate and wistful things have abandoned loveliness for fructifying—the laurel, rank and magnificent for all its tender pink, starts hanging bouquets as big as hydrangeas on its innumerable bushes. But on moonlight nights there's no use trying to say it isn't a glory and a madness! And so the summer starts—summer, when we're not seraph-eyed enough to see flowers even if there were any. In the fall, when our souls return, a little worse off, a little snivelly, there are foggy wisps of asters whose quality only a spider would hint at aloud, and in the streams where the iris forgathered there are parnassia, the snowdrop's only kin. Mountain-folk alone have seen their virginal processions, ankle-deep in water, among scarlet leaves, each holding a round green shield and carrying at the end of a spear, no thicker than a broomstraw, a single pale green star. Last, chilly and inaccessible and sorrowful, in the damp of the deep woods, come the gentians, sea-blue and hushed.

Now all these delights the Arcadians not infrequently neglect. You might stroll across the campus and quadrangles of a sunny afternoon and guess from the emptiness and warm quiet there that they had gone out among the trees, lying perhaps in shadow, idly, like fauns, and whistling at the sky. Some may be so unoccupied, though not faun-like to themselves. But more I fear will be amiably and discreetly behind closed doors on the third floor, playing not flutes or lyres or even saxophones, but poker. Still others will be bowed over a table, vexed to the soul with the return of Xenophon or the fall, too long delayed, of a certain empire. A few will be off in the valley bargaining for a beverage called mountain-dew with a splendid virile old vixen who in that way has always earned a pleasant livelihood. Later they will have consumed their purchase to the last sprightly drop and will be bawling out deplorable ballads and pounding tables and putting crockery to uncouth noisy uses in the neighborhood of one or another of the old ladies, who will appear scandalized as expected, but who in the privacy of her own chamber will laugh soundlessly till her glasses fall off on her bosom and have to be wiped with a handkerchief smelling of orris-root.

Yet I would not have you think that the Arcadians are all or always ribald. Even those with a bacchic turn are full of grace and on occasion given to marvels. I myself have witnessed one of them in the ghastly dawn, slippered and unpantalooned, his chaplet a wet towel, sitting in the corner of his room, his feet against the wall, quite alone, reading in a loud boomy voice more beautiful than chimes *Kubla Khan* and the *Ode to a Nightingale*. One afternoon of thick yellow sunshine I was audience to another who stood on an abandoned windlass with tulip trees and a blue vista for backdrop reciting pentameters, which though you may never have heard, we thought too rich and cadenced for the race of men ever to forget. I can remember them even now for you:

> I dreamed last night of a dome of beaten gold
> To be a counter-glory to the Sun.
> There shall the eagle blindly dash himself,
> There the first beam shall strike, and there the Moon
> Shall aim all night her argent archery;
> And it shall be the tryst of sundered stars,
> The haunt of dead and dreaming Solomon;
> Shall send a light upon the lost in hell,
> And flashings upon faces without hope—
> And I will think in gold and dream in silver,
> Imagine in marble and in bronze conceive,
> Till it shall dazzle pilgrim nations
> And stammering tribes from undiscovered lands,
> Allure the living God out of the bliss,
> And all the streaming seraphim from heaven.

Perhaps a poet whose dear words have died should be content if once, no matter how briefly, they have made two lads in a green-wood more shimmery and plumed.

Nights, spring nights in special, temper and tune the Arcadian soul to very gracious tintinnabulations. Three Arcadians on one occasion, I recall, sat through the setting of one constellation after another on a cliff in the tender moonlight with a breathing sea of gray and silver treetops beneath them and discussed the possibility and probability of God. One, upholding the affirmative, announced that he needed no proof of divinity beyond the amethyst smudge on the horns of the moon. This was countered by the fact that this purple lay not in the moon itself but in the observer's eyes. The deist, troubled, at last concluded anyway he'd rather be a god looking out than look out at a god. Only this was all said with humor and a glistening eagerness—a sort of speech I could once fall into, but long ago.

Myself one of these mountain dwellers for four years, I have observed them, off and on, for thirty more. It is to be marveled at that they never change. They may not be quite the same faces or the precise bodies you met a few years back, but the alterations are ir-relevant—a brown eye instead of a blue one, a nose set a little more to the left. The lining is the same. Neither from experience nor ob-servation can I quite say what they learn in their Arcadia, though they gad about freely with books and pads. Indeed, many of them attempt to assume a studious air by wearing black Oxford gowns. In this they are not wholly successful, for, no matter how new, the gowns always manage to be torn and in-sist on hanging from the supple shoulders with something of a dionysiac abandon. Fur-ther, even the most bookish are given to pur-suing their studies out under the trees. To lie under a tree on your back, overhead a blue and green and gold pattern meddled with by the idlest of breezes, is not—despite the admirable example of Mr. Newton—conducive to the acquisition of knowledge. Flat on your stomach and propped on both elbows, you will inevitably keel and end by doting on the tint of the far shadows, or, worse, by slipping into those delightful oscillations of consciousness known as cat-naps. I cannot therefore commend them for erudition. So it is all the more surprising that in after years the world esteems many of them learned or powerful or godly, and that not infrequently they have been the chosen servitors of the destinies. Yet what they do or know is always less than what they are. Once one of them appeared on the first page of the newspapers because he had climbed with amazing pluck and calculated foolhardiness a hitherto unconquered mountain peak, an Indian boy his only companion. But what we who loved him like best to recall about that exploit is an inch cube of a book he carried along with him and read through—for the hundredth time, likely—before the climb was completed. It was *Hamlet*. Another is immortal for cleansing the world of yellow fever, but the ignorant half-breeds among whom he worked remember him now only for his gentleness, his directness without bluntness, his courtesy which robbed obedience of all humiliation. Still others I understand have amassed fortunes and—to use a word much reverenced by my temporal co-tenants—succeeded. That success I suspect was in spite of their sojourn in our greenwoods. The Arcadians learn here—and that is why I am having such difficulty telling you these things—the imponderables. Ears slightly more pointed and tawny-furred, a bit of leafiness somewhere in the eyes, a manner vaguely Apriline—such attributes though unmistakable are not to be described. When the Arcadians are fools, as they sometimes are, you do not deplore their stupidity, and when they are brilliant you do not resent their intellectuality. The reason is, their manners —the kind not learned or instilled but happening, the core being sweet—are far realer than their other qualities. Socrates and Jesus and St. Francis and Sir Philip Sidney and Lovelace and Stevenson had charm; the Arcadians are of that lineage.

What Pan and Dionysos and the old ladies dower them with is supplemented by an influence which must appear to the uninitiated incompatible. By the aid of a large bell jangled over their sleeping heads from the hands of a perambulating Negro, the Arcadians at seven each morning are driven, not without maledictions, to divine service. A minute before the chapel bell stops ringing, if you happen to be passing, you may imagine the building to be on fire, for young men are dashing to it from every corner of the campus, many struggling with a collar or tie or tightening a belt in their urgent flight. But at the opening of the first hymn you'll find them inside, seated in rows, as quiet as love-birds on a perch. More quiet, in fact: as the service progresses you might well mistake their vacuity for devotion unless you happen to notice the more nocturnal souls here and there who, sagging decorously, have let the warm sleep in.

Nevertheless, the Arcadians add to their list of benefactors those elderly gentlemen about King James who mistranslated certain Hebrew chronicles and poems into the most magnificent music the human tongue has ever syllabled. In their litanies should be named no less those others (or were they the same?) who wrote the Book of Common Prayer. Each morning these young men hear floating across their semi-consciousness the sea-surge of their own language at its most exalted—clean and thunderous and salty. Some of the wash of that stormy splendor lodges in their gay shallows, inevitably and eternally. Who could hear each morning that phrase "the beauty of holiness" without being beguiled into starrier austerities? If someone daily wished that the peace of God and the fellowship of the Holy Ghost might be with you always, could it help sobering and comforting you, even if God to you were only a graybearded old gentleman and the Holy Ghost a dove? Suppose you had never rambled from the divine path farther than the wild-rose hedge along its border, still would not the tide of pity for the illness of things rise in your heart at hearing: "We have wandered and strayed from Thy ways like lost sheep"? Lusty Juventus hereabouts may reflect and forget that there was a modern spiciness in the domestic difficulties of David, but it treasures unforgettably: "The heavens declare the glory of God, and the firmament sheweth His handiwork," and "He maketh me to lie down in green pastures, He leadeth me beside the still waters." Such glistening litter is responsible, perhaps, for the tremulous awe and reverence you find in the recesses of the Arcadian soul—at least you can find them if you are wary and part very gently the sun-spotted greenery of Pan.

Girders and foundations are fine things; and necessary, no doubt. It is stated on authority that the creaking old world would fly into bits without them. But after all what I like best is a tower window. This hankering is an endless source of trouble to me and I like to think to myself, in defense, that it comes from having lived too long among mountain-folk. For they seem always to be leaning from the top of their tower, busy with idle things; watching the leaves shake in the sunlight, the clouds tumble their soundless bales of purple down the long slopes, the seasons eternally up to tricks of beauty, laughing at things that only distance and height reveal humor in, and talking, talking, talking —the enchanting unstained silver of their voices spilling over the bright branches down into the still and happy coves. Sometimes you of the valley may not recognize them, though without introduction they are known of each other. But if some evening a personable youth happens in on your hospitality, greets you with the not irreverent informality reserved for uncles, puts the dowager Empress of Mozambique, your houseguest, at her ease, flirts with your daughter, says grace before the evening meal with unsmiling piety, consumes every variety of food and drink set before him (specializing on hot biscuits) with unabashed gusto, leaves a wake of laughter whenever he dips into the conversation, pays special and apparently delighted attention to the grandmother on his left, enchants the serving maid with two bits and a smile, offers everyone a cigarette, affable under the general disapproval, sings without art a song without merit, sits at last on the doorstep in the moonlight, utterly content, with the dreamy air of the young Hermes (which only means the sense of impending adventure is about his hair like green leaves), and then if that night you dream of a branch of crab-apple blossoms dashed with rain—pursue that youth and entreat him kindly. He hails from Arcady.

COMPOSITION AND
LETTERPRESS PRINTING IN BELL TYPE BY
THE PRESS OF A. COLISH, MOUNT VERNON,
NEW YORK. BINDING BY
PUBLISHERS BOOK BINDERY, INC.,
LONG ISLAND CITY,
NEW YORK.

TYPOGRAPHY BY JERRY KELLY

DATE DUE

DATE DUE			
APR 1 3 1993			
MAY 0 6 1993			
MAR 0 4 1995			
NOV 0 7 1998			
APR 0 9 2004			
GAYLORD			PRINTED IN U.S.A.